TIMEOUT
for Jesus

ENDORSEMENTS

"Timeout for Jesus is a powerful and practical tool for daily meditation. Heather Norman Smith uses varied approaches to expertly accomplish the goal of pointing the reader to Jesus. Each of the thirty readings brings loving challenge and joyful encouragement to help Christians draw closer to Christ. Make sure to make room for Timeout for Jesus in your life!"

-Keith Nix, Lead Pastor of The Lift Church, International Speaker, and Author
www.KeithNix.org

"Timeout for Jesus invites readers to set aside reflective moments to relate with Scripture in the personal corners of their hearts. Heather Norman Smith's gentle words draw us into an intimate conversation around the loving encouragement of Scripture. I love the daily opportunities she provides to "take more time" and consider our relationship with Christ. I highly recommend this lovely, relatable devotional work."

-Tina Yeager, Award-winning Author, Speaker, Podcast Host, LMHC, and Life Coach
www.tinayeager.com

Timeout for Jesus

Thirty Appointments with the Savior

Heather N. Smith

Every Season Books

Copyright © 2019 Heather Norman Smith

All rights reserved.

ISBN: 978-1-7340124-0-8

Scripture quotations marked "NKJV" are taken from the New King James Version. Copyright © 1982 by Thomas Nelson, Inc. All rights reserved. Used by permission.

Scripture quotations marked "ESV" are from the Holy Bible, English Standard Version, copyright © 2001, 2007, 2011, 2016 by Crossway Bibles, a division of Good News Publishers. Used by permission. All rights reserved.

Scripture quotations marked "KJV" are from the King James Version.

Copy Edited by Amy Grochowski.

Published by Every Season Books.

To all the seekers.

Ask, and it shall be given you; seek, and ye shall find; knock, and it shall be opened unto you...

Matthew 7:7 (KJV)

CONTENTS

	Introduction	
1	Everything You Will Ever Need	1
2	Do You Have a Birthmark?	4
3	To Take Up Space	7
4	Higher Ground	10
5	The Key to Abundant Living	13
6	Big Power in Little Prayers	16
7	Pass Me Not	20
8	All Things	24
9	Five Reasons You Are Awesome	27
10	Speaking Blessing to Others	31
11	Disciple is a Verb	34
12	To Be or Not to Be	37
13	Come Into The Light	40
14	His Abiding Presence	43
15	Feeding Like the Birds	46
16	The "Him" of His Garment	49
17	How I'm Like My Dog…	52

18	What's Your Motivation?	55
19	A List for Guiding Your Thoughts	58
20	Where Will You Find Yourself Next?	62
21	The Clear Glass Mosaic	66
22	Breath	69
23	If My Bible Disappeared	72
24	Sent Away by Jesus	75
25	Invitation Etiquette	79
26	Time to Look Back	82
27	The Real Root of All Evil	85
28	Praying from the Word	89
29	Schools of Fish and Jesus-Followers	92
30	Are You Where You Thought You'd Be?	96
	Closing Prayer	99

INTRODUCTION

Timeout for Jesus. No, this title doesn't imply disciplinary measures for the perfect, spotless, sinless son of God. Neither is it a sports metaphor. Instead, we are taking time out of our hectic lives, purposefully, *for* Him—to meditate on His goodness, reflect on His grace, and invite Him into our busyness.

If you have children, you may have tried to correct undesired behaviors with a firm, "Sit here and think about what you've done." Or, chances are, those words have been directed toward you at some point in your life. The purpose of this devotional is not to think about what we've done, bad or good. I invite you to take a timeout to sit and think about what He has done. And I assure you, all of it is good.

These devotions were selected and edited from several years of blog posts on my website. Some are long, others short. Some read like a Bible study chapter, and others are more poetic and reflective. But I pray each will be what you need at the right time and will be a helpful supplement to your regular quiet time with God. Thank you for reading.

1

Everything You Will Ever Need

According as his divine power hath given unto us all things that pertain unto life and godliness, through the knowledge of him that hath called us to glory and virtue...

2 Peter 1:3 (KJV)

There are some big promises in the Word of God, and I think we sometimes miss them. Maybe we get so caught up trying to fill our scripture quota we miss the truth of what God is saying. But I've found a big promise, wrapped up in two itty-bitty words: *All things*. God has promised us **EVERYTHING** we will ever need.

The Bible says that God has given us all things that pertain to life and godliness through the knowledge of Jesus[1]. He has given us everything! That's a big thought. When we know Jesus, we are fully equipped with all the things we need, not only to live, but to live godly lives.

---

[1] 2 Peter 1:3 (KJV)

The promise of total sufficiency through God began in the Garden of Eden. Genesis 9:3 (KJV) says, "Every moving thing that liveth shall be meat for you; even as the green herb have I given you all things." This is an example of God not holding any good thing back. He provided completely.

The idea of abundance in Christ has nothing to do with a prosperity gospel. That's a very narrow way to look at the blessings of God. The Bible says, "Charge them that are rich in this world, that they be not highminded, nor trust in uncertain riches, but in the living God, who giveth us richly all things to enjoy."[2] What does *all things* mean? What exactly do we have? I believe it means literally everything. We have access to everything we could possibly need or want, according to His will. The sky is the limit—if God wills it. And if He doesn't will it, I don't want it!

Part of a beautiful sermon from the Apostle Paul says, "God that made the world and all things therein, seeing that he is Lord of heaven and earth, dwelleth not in temples made with hands; Neither is worshipped with men's hands, as though he needed any thing, seeing he giveth to all life, and breath, and all things."[3]

God made everything; He owns everything; and, He gives everything to us as His children. What more could we possibly want? When you have Jesus,

---

[2] 1 Timothy 6:17 (KJV)
[3] Acts 17:24,25 (KJV)

you have everything.

> **Take more time**
>
> Check out these other applicable "all things" verses: Romans 8:28 (my favorite); Psalm 8:6; Philippians 4:13; Matthew 19:26; Matthew 6:33; 1 Corinthians 3:21.

Prayer

Lord, help me to trust in Your sufficiency. Thank you for being my Everything.

2

DO YOU HAVE A BIRTHMARK?

That which is born of the flesh is flesh; and that which is born of the Spirit is spirit.

John 3:6 (KJV)

I have an insignificant deformity on the top of my left ear. It's not very noticeable, and I hardly ever think about it. But it's been part of me since I was born. My birthmark.

My three kids have their own marks. Each has a small brown circle on their skin: the oldest on her leg, the middle on her back, and the baby on his arm. I've always been fascinated by these birthmarks—how similar but different they are, what causes them, and why we have them.

The Bible says that to be a follower of Christ, you must be born *again*,[1] and that spiritual birth also comes with a mark—something that brands us as believers and sets us apart from the rest of the world.

---

[1] John 3:3

When we are born again, the Holy Spirit takes up residence within us, and He changes us.

Galatians 5:22-23 teaches that the fruits of the Holy Spirit in a person's life are:

- *Love*
- *Joy*
- *Peace*
- *Patience*
- *Kindness*
- *Goodness*
- *Faithfulness*
- *Gentleness*
- *Self-control*

These are definite birthmarks that set us apart, yet still we struggle with flesh. After all, these traits aren't known as the Fruits of the Believer. The Spirit plants them, and we are responsible to grow them through a relationship with Jesus. That means spending time in the Word and in prayer. The more I pray, the more self-control and faithfulness I have. The more I read the Bible, the more love and joy I have. You get the picture. As the fruit grows, it becomes more noticeable to the world around us. It's our mark. A sign of our new birth. Strive to show someone your birthmark today.

> **Take more time**
>
> Think about it. What shape are your spiritual birthmarks? Meaning, how do the fruits of the Spirit affect your life? Maybe you lacked gentleness or kindness prior to accepting Christ. Have your relationships improved because of spiritual fruit?

Prayer

Lord, help me to walk in the Spirit and not the flesh, so others may see the evidence of my new birth. May You be glorified by my life.

3

To Take Up Space

Therefore, to him who knows to do good and does not do it, to him it is sin.

James 4:17 (NKJV)

Do you remember journaling time in school? Or maybe it was called free writing. I recall being given a thin, dull-white piece of paper with faint pink and blue lines and a pencil as big around as my thumb, and being told to write something in fifteen minutes to be reviewed later by my first-grade teacher. We could write about anything—a new toy, a made-up story, what we wanted to be when we grew up. Most days, I loved it. Some days, there were no good thoughts in my head, yet I had to fill the paper. On more than one occasion, my work looked something like this:

I am writing to take up space.

I have to use all the lines, so I am writing these words to take up space on the paper.

I can't think of anything to write about except that I have nothing to write about.

You get the idea. I thought it was a clever way to solve my problem, but I don't think Mrs. Collins agreed.

I think about those writing assignments often—how the paper ripped when I was overzealous with the eraser and how intimidating those solid and dotted lines could be. Mostly, the image of that familiar paper reminds me how I don't want to live my life. I don't want to live the way I wrote when the inspiration wouldn't come. I don't want to live just to take up space. I pray God will help me be more than a consumer of oxygen in this earth, and help me produce something meaningful and beautiful with the resources I've been given.

The Bible says, "Whereas you do not know what will happen tomorrow. For what is your life? It is even a vapor that appears for a little time and then vanishes away."[1] There are a finite amount of lines on the page, and pencils eventually get sharpened to nubs. We must be mindful to make the writing assignment of life more than vain words.

Write a good story. Fill the lines on the page well. Don't live just to fill the space between the margins of birth and death. Actively seek to do good. One day, the Teacher will review our work. May it be our best effort, with His help.

---

[1] James 4:14 (NKJV)

> **Take more time**
>
> Have you ever had a dream to do good? Think of something altruistic you've always imagined but never got around to doing. Maybe it's foster care, feeding the homeless, or volunteering at a hospital. Whatever it is, ask God to help you take the first step today.

Prayer

Thank you, Lord, for another day of life.
Help me make this one count for You.

4

Higher Ground

Hear my cry, O God; attend unto my prayer. From the end of the earth will I cry unto thee, when my heart is overwhelmed: lead me to the rock that is higher than I.

Psalm 61:1-2 (KJV)

The images on the news told a heartbreaking story. People in Houston, Texas walked through flooded streets, some with belongings lifted high over their heads, as they tried to escape the devastating effects of Tropical Storm Harvey. They looked so helpless and desperate, overwhelmed by water. The pained look on each face made my heart ache, and I prayed for their safety. "Oh, if they could just get to higher ground!" I thought.

I don't know much about the landscape of Houston. I think of Texas as being very flat. And with the water coming down so fast, it seemed their only refuge would be an elevated place.

Many times, in life, we feel flooded with trouble, much like the literal flood experienced in The Lone Star State. It rains down on us and overtakes us, and we are desperate to get to a place of refuge.

King David certainly felt like this when he said, "Lead me to the rock that is higher than I."[1] There is a Rock that is higher than all of us, a place of spiritual safety above the storms of life.

When we trust Him, God is our rock. The Word says, "In God is my salvation and my glory: the rock of my strength, and my refuge, is in God."[2]

Rocks are solid. They provide stability. In the New Testament, Jesus compares those who follow His teaching to "a wise man, which built his house upon a rock: And the rain descended, and the floods came, and the winds blew, and beat upon that house; and it fell not: for it was founded upon a rock."[3]

The Word of God provides a sure foundation for life. No matter what circumstances we face, we can trust in the Bible to point us in the right direction and teach us how to endure trials.

I pray for people in the path of a storm today—real or metaphorical. I pray God will provide safety and refuge.

If you feel overwhelmed, trust in Him as your Rock. Let Him comfort your heart and give you courage.

---

[1] Psalm 61:2 (KJV)
[2] Psalm 62:7 (KJV)
[3] Matthew 7:24-25 (KJV)

Take more time

Think of a time in your life when you trusted God as your refuge, then think of a time when you didn't. How much better did the situation turn out when you sought God's help?

Prayer

Lord, thank you for being my Higher Ground. Help me to put my trust in You no matter what life brings.

5

The Key to Abundant Living

And to know the love of Christ, which passeth knowledge, that ye might be filled with all the fulness of God.

Ephesians 3:19 (KJV)

I remember well the day I spent a couple hours floating down a peaceful river on an innertube surrounded by majestic scenery, under a sunny sky, in the company of kind friends and my two oldest children. The current carried us gently, and the cool water cradled us as we lounged, carefree and basking in nature's beauty. Such a glorious experience. It was the kind of day that makes you feel grateful to exist and in awe of a loving Creator who provides such experiences to His children.

But it made me think. Would I be so grateful if my circumstances were different? Would I still be in awe of the Creator's handiwork without these pleasant days and beautiful landscapes? Would I admire His gifts so much if my world didn't look like this?

I can't answer those questions with certainty,

but I like to think the answer *is—I would.*

Admittedly, I have fears, worries, and doubts, and there are days when I allow my perspective to be skewed. Sometimes, I find myself grumbling and complaining about things that have no real consequence. But even on those days, I have an abiding joy that is the hallmark of an abundant life.

So, what does it mean to live abundantly and how do we do it? One of the definitions for the word abundant is, "richly supplied, as with resources."[1] When I think about that definition, it occurs to me: abundant living is not measured by tangible resources. Living abundantly means having a completeness and fullness in life that does not depend on circumstances. Abundant living is being richly supplied in resources which transcend our natural understanding. The key to abundant living is recognizing the Source.

Jesus said, "I am come that they might have life, and that they might have it more abundantly."[2] Jesus does not merely supply us with abundance. He *is* our abundance. Jesus doesn't simply give us joy. He *is* our joy. As children of God, we must recognize that even the ability to feel the emotions we associate with the idea of abundance comes from Him.

Abundant living comes from fellowship with the God of the universe, through Christ. I can

---

[1] Dictionary.com, s.v., "abundant," accessed August 10, 2019, https://www.diction-ary.com/abdundant
[2] John 10:10b

experience joy and have gratitude for of all the blessings of life—the natural world, the love of my family, my earthly pleasures—but the true source of abundance is the fullness of God.

Did my experience on the river qualify as living abundantly? Sure! But only by extension. It is the relationship I have with God which reveals the truth of His goodness and allows me to enjoy the life He has provided. Having a relationship with God is living abundantly.

 Take more time

Ask yourself some hard questions. If Jesus were all you had, would He be enough? Can life really be full when it's empty of everything besides God? If you struggle with this, pray and ask God to help shape your mindset.

Prayer

Thank you for giving me a life of abundance. God, let my relationship with You be the most fulfilling thing in my life.

6

Big Power in Little Prayers

Pray without ceasing.

1 Thessalonians 5:17 (KJV)

"Your will be done, Lord."

I find myself saying it often—when I'm driving, walking into work, cleaning the house. My mind may be in a million different places, but that phrase will squeeze its way into my thoughts, and I'll direct it to Him.

One day while listening to a sermon on the radio, God spoke to my spirit about my simple five-word petition. He confirmed that each time I whispered that prayer, He received it and acted on my behalf. He orders my steps, in part, because of my feeble request for His will to be done. How wonderful that even little prayers are answered by our big God!

Let's look at three short prayers from the Bible that had great impact.

- "And Samson called unto the LORD, and said, O Lord GOD, remember me, I pray thee, and strengthen me, I pray thee, only this once, O God, that I may be at once avenged of the Philistines for my two eyes."[1]

After his prayer, Samson was given the strength to destroy the temple of Dagon.

- "And, behold, there came a leper and worshipped him, saying, Lord, if thou wilt, thou canst make me clean."[2]

After his prayer, the leper was cleansed.

- "And he said unto Jesus, Lord, remember me when thou comest into thy kingdom."[3]

After his prayer, the thief was promised eternal life.

In all three examples, the petitions were granted even though the words spoken were few. It didn't take great orations or lengthy invocations to move the heart of God. When it comes to prayer, quality is more important than quantity, and what qualifies a prayer as effective is the faith behind it.

For sure, the more we can pray with faith, the better! I strive daily to spend more time in prayer.

---

[1] Judges 16:28 (KJV)
[2] Matthew 8:2 (KJV)
[3] Luke 23:42 (KJV)

There are so many things about which to pray—our families, our nation and leaders, our churches, our spiritual growth, and our non-believing loved ones. And those are just requests. We could spend 24/7 offering prayers of thanksgiving and praise! But don't discount those quick prayers uttered as you go about your day. The Bible says, "Pray without ceasing."[4] I think that can look like this:

Lord, help me on this test.

Please bless my children.

Make me more like You.

Give us opportunities to show Your love.

Thank you.

I'm so glad God hears and responds to "little" prayers, as well as the "big" ones.

---

[4] 1 Thessalonians 5:17

> **Take more time**
>
> Read another well-known prayer from the Bible—the prayer of Jabez in 1 Chronicles 4:10.

Prayer

Teach me to pray without ceasing, Lord. May You be a constant presence in my heart and mind. Thank You for hearing all my prayers—big and small.

7

Pass Me Not

For I say, through the grace given to me, to everyone who is among you, not to think of himself more highly than he ought to think, but to think soberly, as God has dealt to each one a measure of faith.

Romans 12:3 (NKJV)

While the Holy Scriptures are the only divine texts we possess, I believe God has inspired people throughout the ages to write songs to be used for His glory. He uses these songs to speak to us.

One day, while driving to a coffee shop for a mid-day treat, I began singing the old hymn, "Pass Me Not, O Gentle Savior." This song was written by one of God's greatest poets—Fanny Crosby—and it has a beautiful melody, composed by William Doane in 1870.

Pass me not, O gentle Savior,
Hear my humble cry;
While on others Thou art calling,
Do not pass me by.

Savior, Savior,
Hear my humble cry,
While on others Thou art calling,
Do not pass me by.

As I drove, I reflected on the lyrics, and it began to bother me. Was it really okay to plead for God not to pass me by, as if He would *actually* do such a thing? Later, I sought the origin of the hymn to help resolve the question, and the internet proved very helpful. An article by a professor of sacred music stated that the inspiration for the song was a visit to a prison by Crosby during the Spring of 1868. It is believed that after the poet had spoken and her hymns had been sung, she heard one of the prisoners cry out in a pleading voice, "Good Lord, do not pass me by."

This prisoner sounds like a man who had enough faith to understand he needed God, but was not yet acquainted with God enough to know he could trust Him. He reminds me of the father in the book of Mark, chapter 9, who, wanting Jesus to heal his son, proclaimed, "Lord, I believe; help thou mine unbelief."[1] That story gives me such hope. Although the man admitted to having a measure of unbelief, Jesus healed his son based on the measure of faith he *did* have. (The last line of the second verse of "Pass Me Not, O Gentle Savior" is "Help my unbelief.")

The tone of the song also reminds me of King

---

[1] Mark 9:24 (KJV)

David and how he pleaded with God in despair, yet he ended his petition with a praise acknowledging God's faithfulness. In one part he says, "How long wilt thou forget me, O LORD? for ever? how long wilt thou hide thy face from me?"[2] But, just five versus later he says, "I will sing unto the LORD, because he hath dealt bountifully with me."[3] Even a man well-acquainted with the provision of God, who is described as a man after God's own heart[4], struggled with whether or not God would be present in his situation. But because of His knowledge of the nature of God, he could ultimately be at peace.

After some soul-searching, I was reassured. The words "do not pass me by" are an expression of every sincere heart which has longed to be close to the Almighty, yet in human frailty can hardly comprehend that the God of the universe lends His availability and concern to sinners such as us. How kind and compassionate our God is to His creation.

---

[2] Psalm 13:1 (KJV)
[3] Psalm 13:6 (KJV)
[4] Acts 13:22

> **Take more time**
>
> Can you think of another special hymn that causes you to reflect on the goodness of God? Find a quiet place and sing it as an offering of praise to Him.

Prayer

Lord, help my unbelief. Thank you for being a God of mercy and compassion. Help me not to forget that You are ever-faithful.

8

All Things

And we know that all things work together for good to them that love God, to them who are the called according to His purpose.

Romans 8:28 (KJV)

As I tried to sleep, somewhere amid the rambling, disjointed thoughts flooding my tired brain, I recognized one of my favorite verses. I didn't consciously think of Romans 8:28, but it was suddenly there in my mind. The familiar words had barely finished processing when they were followed by a simple question: *Do you know?*

Whether it was me asking the question or the Holy Spirit, I had to ponder. *Do I really know that all things work together for good? Do I believe it with certainty?* Yes, I believe it with all my heart. But the real question was and is, do I live like I know it? Do you?

The phrase *all things* in this verse could mean literally everything—from a walk to the mailbox to a serious illness. While I believe Romans 8:28 is true for "all" circumstances, Paul was writing about persecution. With that context in mind, we should examine how we perceive difficulties.

Knowing that all things work together for good doesn't mean we never hurt or have concerns about the difficult times in life. Our state of salvation doesn't preclude us from the effects of living in a fallen world. Bad things will happen—although I believe we are guarded by His sovereign grace from many bad circumstances. The beauty of knowing that *all things work together for good* is summed up in one word: hope. We have hope that beauty will be born of brokenness and silver linings will surface through stress. And we can learn to even be excited when something bad happens, anticipating the good that will come from it. Sometimes, we may not see the good, but by faith we know it is there, because God's promises are true. It's not about learning to see the glass as half full instead of half empty. There are plenty of atheist optimists. But it's about knowing that God is intentionally acting and working things out in all situations and about being able to praise Him whether we see the good or not.

Let me give you a real-life example. A small, country church where my husband ministered for a season was vandalized. On an Easter Sunday morning, the congregants found a swastika spray-painted on the front door. Now, of course, that's not a good thing. How could it be? But the deputy who responded to the call did a *wonderful* thing—he painted over the vandalism, without being asked, on the spot. Our friends were deeply moved by the kind act, and they took to social media to praise the officer. More than one news station saw the post and reached out for an interview. God worked it out for the story to be shared and encourage many people!

Because our friends knew God was in control of the situation, they focused on the deputy's good deed instead of the wrong done to them. Perhaps the best is yet to come from their story.

Have you been going through a trial? Are you facing adversity now? God can and will use it for good. Perhaps the best is yet to come from your story, too.

 Take more time

Let your imagination run wild. In what ways might God work out your situation for good? What unseen benefit could come from hard times? Anything is possible. But God's plan will always be even greater than we can imagine.

Prayer

Thank you, God, for this big, wonderful promise from Your Word. Help me to believe it without exception.

9

Five Reasons You Are Awesome

I will praise thee; for I am fearfully and wonderfully made: marvelous are thy works; and that my soul knoweth right well.

Psalm 139:14 (KJV)

It seems as if every mainstream web article these days is written in list format. *10 Secrets to Perfect Homemade Pizza. 7 Fabulous Vacation Ideas. The Top 5 Reasons to Own a Pet.* People like lists. So, I'm going to give you the best list you will read today: *5 Reasons YOU Are Awesome!*

1.) YOU were created in the image of God.

The Bibles says, "And God said, Let us make man in our image, after our likeness: and let them have dominion over the fish of the sea, and over the fowl of the air, and over the cattle, and over all the earth, and over every creeping thing that creepeth upon the earth. So God created man in his *own* image, in the image of God created he him; male and female created he them."[1]

You are awesome because you are modeled after the Creator of the universe. Not only did God make us in His image, He gave us authority over and responsibility for the earth.

2.) YOU are a work of art!

When God was finished sculpting the earth and everything in it, including humankind, He thought it was very good.[2] You are His masterpiece!

There's a saying, attributed to the late singer Ethel Waters: "I am somebody 'cause God don't make no junk!" While not grammatically correct, the statement is profoundly wise. We can be assured of our awesomeness, because our Creator is perfect.

3.) YOU were born for a purpose!

The Scriptures indicate that God gives people specific life missions. There's a reason you are here, even if you never fully figure out what it is.

God told the prophet Jeremiah, "Before I formed thee in the belly I knew thee; and before thou camest forth out of the womb I sanctified thee, and I ordained thee a prophet unto the nations."[3] Likewise, the apostle Paul said, "But when it pleased God, who

---

[1] Genesis 1:26-27 (KJV)
[2] Genesis 1:31
[3] Jeremiah 1:5

separated me from my mother's womb, and called me by his grace...."[4] Paul had a job to do for the Lord, long before he knew about it.

Rest in the fact that He did not place you on earth *just because*. You have a purpose.

4.) Jesus Died For YOU.

If you ever doubt your value, just remember that Christ paid the highest price to save you. You are so valuable, He gave His own life for you.

Romans 5:8 (KJV) says, "But God commendeth his love toward us, in that, while we were yet sinners, Christ died for us." And you probably know John 3:16, which speaks of God's love and Christ's sacrifice.

5.) IF you have accepted Jesus as your Savior, YOU have the Spirit of God living in you.

This one is of course conditional. But if you are part of the family of God, you have the gift of His Spirit. The Holy Spirit lives in all believers and produces spiritual fruit[5] and bestows spiritual gifts[6] akin to superpowers!

The Holy Spirit also teaches you[7] and helps

---

[4] Galatians 1:15
[5] Galatians 5:22-23
[6] Romans 12:6-8
[7] John 14:26

you witness to others.[8]

I'm sure there are many, many more reasons why and ways you are awesome. But now that we are feeling good about ourselves, let's put this into perspective. You are awesome. But we are nothing without Him. John (the Baptizer) said "He must increase, but I must decrease."[9] Hold your head high today and know how valuable you are in Him, but remember to give Him glory for your awesomeness.

 Take more time

Do you know someone who needs a confidence boost? Pick one or more of these five reasons to share with them. Honor God with a gift of encouraging others.

Prayer

God, you are glorious and wonderful, righteous and holy. I worship you for being an awesome God.

---

[8] Matthew 10:20
[9] John 3:30 (KJV)

10

Speaking Blessing to Others

Death and life are in the power of the tongue: and they that love it shall eat the fruit thereof.

Proverbs 18:21 (KJV)

What does it mean to bless someone? When you bless someone, you are speaking good things into existence in their lives. Did you realize you have that kind of power? We bless people by claiming a promise from the Bible on their behalf.

In the Old Testament, God gave the priests of Israel a specific blessing to use:

"This is the way you shall bless the children of Israel. Say to them:

'The Lord bless you and keep you;
The Lord make His face shine upon you,
And be gracious to you;
The Lord lift up His countenance upon you,
And give you peace.'

So they shall put My name on the children of Israel, and I will bless them."[1]

---

[1] Numbers 6:23b-27 (NKJV)

The Bible teaches that, through Jesus, we are adopted into the family of God and all the promises He gave to Israel are for us, too.[2] That means we can use this same blessing.

Sometimes before we head out to face the world, I speak something like this for each of my children: "The Lord bless you and keep you and give you a good day, in Jesus' name." They've told me it helps.

Speaking blessing is a lot like praying, but instead of asking God for something, we are claiming something He already promised. A blessing must line up with the Bible. We know God is not a magic genie that grants wishes, so I wouldn't say to someone, "May the Lord give you a million dollars." The Bible doesn't promise us a million dollars. But it does promise good things like peace when we need it. So, I could say, "May the Lord give you peace," and that is a blessing God will honor and work through, because He's already promised it.[3]

At the close of Paul's first letter to the Corinthians, he wrote, "The grace of our Lord Jesus Christ be with you."[4] He blessed them with that statement.

Some blessings are very simple. We often say, "God bless you." Especially at church. It can even become habit, and we say it without meaning.

---

[2] Galatians 3-4
[3] John 14:27
[4] 1 Corinthians 16:23 (KJV)

But any time we use the name of God, we should use it with intention. Think about what you're saying next time, and really mean it! When we have faith that God will actually help someone and give them what they need, those three words are very powerful!

Practice speaking blessing to someone in your life today.

 Take more time

Search the Scriptures for more blessings to speak:
- 1 Thessalonians 3:12-13
- 1 Thessalonians 5:23
- 2 Timothy 4:22
- Hebrews 13:20-21

Prayer

Thank you, Lord, for the power we have through You. Remind me to bless others and not curse them. Give me opportunities to lift others up, in Your will.

11

Disciple is a Verb

I press toward the mark for the prize of the high calling of God in Christ Jesus.

Philippians 3:14 (KJV)

I love words. As someone who has always enjoyed writing, I value the meaning of words. I appreciate the dictionary, and I use it regularly to make sure I am using words correctly.

Doing a little study, I found something in an online dictionary that surprised me. Two of the definitions for the verb form of *disciple*, were listed as *archaic* and *obsolete*, respectively. Three online dictionaries I checked didn't have *disciple* listed as a verb at all. Although mostly used as a noun, I believe *disciple* is an action word, too!

For the sake of clarity, *disciple* is not used in the Bible as a verb, either. But the meaning is certainly there. Discipleship is a long-standing principal of the Christian church, and I think the most direct scriptural reference is found in what we call, "The Great Commission."

"And Jesus came and spake unto them, saying, 'All power is given unto me in heaven and in earth. Go ye therefore, and teach all nations, baptizing them in the name of the Father, and of the Son, and of the Holy Ghost: Teaching them to observe all things whatsoever I have commanded you: and, lo, I am with you always, even unto the end of the world."[1]

The part that stands out to me is "teaching them to observe all things whatsoever I have commanded you." The definition listed online as *obsolete* was "to teach; train."[2] It's sad that something so explicitly given as a command in the Great Commission is considered obsolete with regard to modern-day usage. The definition listed online as *archaic* was "to convert into a disciple."[3]

We are called to teach people about Jesus so that they choose to follow Him; then we continue to teach them the truth of His Word, so they can live according to His commandments and lead others in that same knowledge.

Challenge yourself to promote *disciple* as a verb in the common English lexicon by putting your faith into action. We are not just disciples (noun.) We are called *to disciple* (verb), meaning to make disciples of others!

---

[1] Matthew 28:18-20 (KJV)
[2] Dictionary.com, s.v., "disciple," accessed August 13, 2019, https://www.diction-ary.com/disciple
[3] Dictionary.com, s.v., "disciple," accessed August 13, 2019, https://www.diction-ary.com/disciple

We may not personally go to "all nations," but discipleship can start with those closest to you. The most convenient opportunities for discipleship are in our own homes. Our families are a prime audience for speaking the truth of the Gospel. If you are a parent, do your best to teach your children His word, with His help.

 Take more time

Think about it: In what ways can you disciple someone personally? What organizations can you support that disciple people around the world?

Prayer

Heavenly Father, I can do nothing in my own strength. Teach me to be a good disciple. Help me disciple others well, for Your glory.

12

To Be or Not To Be

For we have not an high priest which cannot be touched with the feeling of our infirmities; but was in all points tempted like as we are, yet without sin.

Hebrews 4:15 (KJV)

Have you ever been reading the Bible and something jumped out at you? Like it leapt off the page (or screen) and said, "Hey! Look at me! You need to get this!" This happened to me while reading the fourth chapter of the book of Matthew. The passage starts out after Jesus was baptized, and the first verse says, "Then was Jesus led up of the Spirit into the wilderness to be tempted of the devil."

Wait a minute. What did that say? Jesus went to the wilderness *to be* tempted? In this very familiar story, those two words had never seemed so important. Jesus went to the wilderness with the specific purpose of being tempted! He didn't go there to meditate and *happened* to be tempted. He wasn't going to fast and pray then Satan showed up and surprised Him. He went there TO BE TEMPTED! It was a revelation to me.

The Lord of all creation, in an earthly body, purposefully subjected himself to real temptation. This is difficult to grasp. I want to rationalize that the time of testing Jesus endured really wasn't much of a test, because Jesus is divine and holy. He has all the power in the universe, so resisting the devil must have been effortless, right? Not quite.

While on the earth, Jesus was 100% God and 100% man at the same time. The math doesn't work at all, but it's still true. His temptation in the wilderness was a deliberate surrendering of His divinity, just like He did on the cross when He became sin for us. He supernaturally slipped on the mantle of natural flesh, so he could relate to me and you in our struggles with temptation.

The Holy Spirit explained it for us through the writing of the Apostle Paul: "For because he himself has suffered when tempted, he is able to help those who are being tempted."[1]

There is so much to learn from the story of the temptation of Christ. There's the example of how to withstand temptation by being spiritually prepared through prayer and fasting. Then there's the example of fighting the devil through the power of the Word. Those are important take-aways. But we should also understand that Christ was tempted willingly, and that He did it for you and me. It was a selfless act of love toward mankind. He wanted to know His creation so intimately that He became flesh and

---

[1] Hebrews 2:18 (ESV)

endured the feelings of temptation as a man.

> **Take more time**
>
> Read Isaiah 53:3. Think about the different emotions Christ felt on our behalf, to redeem us and prove His love for us.

Prayer

Thank you, Jesus, for understanding me so well. Help me to never forget what a good and loving friend You are. May the knowledge of Your sacrifices compel me to live for You always.

13

Come Into The Light

Draw near to God and He will draw near to you. Cleanse your hands, you sinners; and purify your hearts, you double-minded.

James 4:8 (NKJV)

The bright late-May sunshine fell on my face, luxuriously warm. I closed my eyes and let my skin soak up its energy, as the corners of my mouth automatically drew upward in delight. Its rays reinvigorated my weary soul. But it was only for a second. The sun kissed me for a literal second, then it was gone. Back again. Gone again. Back again. Gone again. Over and over.

The swing on the back deck of my house was in just the right spot for me to experience the sunshine on the way up, but the backswing put me in the shadow of the house. I wanted to enjoy the sun, but I was tired, and the obvious solution of moving the swing didn't seem worth the energy.

How often does this happen in my spiritual life? I go back and forth between experiencing *The Light* and slipping into the shadows. I love the benefits of spending time with God, but I don't always make the effort.

To be clear, as a child of God, He's always with me. But because of *my* actions, I'm not always basking in the fullness of relationship with him. And the solution for that is as simple as moving the swing. I need to move myself to do the things that *I know* promote fellowship with God—spending more time in prayer and reading the Word.

We should aim to experience His presence more than only at church or when we need something from Him. His presence should be where we live! The Bible says, "Surely the righteous shall give thanks unto thy name: the upright shall dwell in thy presence."[1]

What are you waiting for? Take a step out of the shadows today. Let's move into the Light.

---

[1] Psalm 140:13

> **Take more time**
>
> Think about ways you can intentionally strengthen your relationship with Jesus. What steps can you take to fit more prayer or Bible reading into your day?

Prayer

Lord, Thank You for never leaving me. Please show me how to draw closer to You today.

14

His Abiding Presence

And, lo, I am with you alway, even unto the end of the world. Amen.

Matthew 28:20b (KJV)

As a society, we're accustomed to constant human interaction. We enjoy the convenience of social media and the instant connection technology allows. What would it be like if it all went away—if social media ceased to exist, if phones were unavailable? It's difficult to imagine. I'd miss my online companions, and it would take a long time to adjust, but I would still have my church, my family, and Jesus.

But let's imagine further. What if, God forbid, my church family dissolved? What if that fellowship was no longer available to me? I would certainly grieve, but I'd still have my family and Jesus.

Though I can barely stand to consider it, what if family weren't with me? What if I was taken to a far-off place, away from everything and everyone I know and love. How horrible! But my soul rests in the fact that I'd still have Jesus.

But what if Jesus…? There are no more what-ifs. Jesus is the only thing in my existence that can't be removed from me, the only thing that is inextricable from my being. While the other situations are, thankfully, improbable, losing Jesus is simply impossible. What an awesome thought—I have something that can never be taken away. As a believer, I have the Spirit of the Living God with me at all times, and He will always be a constant and abiding presence, regardless of any other circumstance in my life.

Psalm 139:7-10 (ESV) says, "Where shall I go from your Spirit? Or where shall I flee from your presence? If I ascend to heaven, you are there! If I make my bed in Sheol, you are there! If I take the wings of the morning and dwell in the uttermost parts of the sea, even there your hand shall lead me, and your right hand shall hold me."

Imagine your surroundings as a silent void, an abyss of nothingness. Even in that place, God is there. And in nothingness, you have abundance as a child of God. There is no fission process that can separate Him from you. No matter where you are, He is there. He will always be there, and He is sufficient.

Take more time

Find a quiet place completely free of distractions. Sit with your eyes closed and try to block out every thought in your mind. Then think on Him. Thank Him for being ever-present.

Prayer

Thank you, Lord, for being with me always, regardless of my circumstances. I love you for being a constant friend.

15

Feeding Like the Birds

For the bread of God is he which cometh down from heaven, and giveth life unto the world.

John 6:33 (KJV)

Over the past few years, I've developed a love and appreciation for birds. I think it's part of getting older—we start slowing down to see things that have been right in front of us all along but were too busy to appreciate. I have a couple of feeders up around my house, and I get joy out of watching the little birds come to eat. One day, I noticed how the different species feed differently than each other, and it made me think of the different ways believers consume spiritual food.

The sparrow hangs out at the feeder, taking its time. It pecks and eats leisurely, perched in the same spot for a long while. Some people spend time with God this way, setting aside quality time to soak up His presence. They are in no hurry.

The chickadees and wrens dart in and grab a bite, then fly away quickly. But they come back soon. Back and forth, they feed throughout the day.

Spiritually, I find myself most like these birds. I spend time with God in short, frequent periods—a verse here and a prayer there, a song lifted as I go about my day.

I also noticed that some of the birds prefer to eat alone, while others usually come with a friend. The cardinals and house finches come in pairs. While Christians are instructed to assemble regularly, some believers get the best spiritual food in their quiet time alone with God. Others thrive on corporate worship.

No matter how you like to be fed, the most important thing is to eat. We may do it differently, but spending time with Jesus through worship, prayer, and reading the Bible, is the spiritual food we all need.

Take more time

We spend a lot of energy trying to identify our personality type or our learning style. Have you ever given though to what type of worshipper you are? Take time to evaluate how you worship "best."

Prayer

Thank you for allowing us to see You in all of Creation. Thank you for feeding the spirit of everyone who comes to You hungry.

16

The "Him" of His Garment

The LORD is my strength and my shield; my heart trusted in him, and I am helped: therefore my heart greatly rejoiceth; and with my song will I praise him.

Psalm 28:7(KJV)

What is the essence of a person? The dictionary defines *essence* as "the properties or attributes by means of which something can be placed in its proper class or identified as being what it is" and "the most significant element, quality, or aspect of a thing or person."[1]

In the book of Matthew, we find a familiar story that describes the essence of Jesus:

"And, behold, a woman, which was diseased with an issue of blood twelve years, came behind him, and touched the hem of his garment: For she said within herself, If I may but touch his garment, I shall be whole. But Jesus turned him about, and when he saw her, he said, Daughter, be of good comfort;

---

[1] "essence." Merriam-Webster.com. 2019. https://www.merriam-webster.com (14 August 2019).

thy faith hath made thee whole. And the woman was made whole from that hour."[2]

As demonstrated in this story from history, a significant part of Jesus' essence is His power. His miracles help us identify Him as God. Certainly, the healing virtue didn't come from the garment. Jesus didn't wear a magical cloak, neither do I believe that His divine power was transferred to the fabric. I believe that if the woman had reached out and come up ten feet short of touching the hem of His garment, she still would have been made whole, because what she grabbed wasn't just the hem of His garment, it was the "Him" of his garment. Her faith wasn't in the clothes. It was in who Jesus was, His identity as God in flesh. And her faith resulted in a miracle.

This story displays not only Jesus' power, but two other traits that describe his essence; He is both omniscient and compassionate. People pressed in from all sides, yet He knew who had reached out in faith. He picked her out of the mob. And He had compassion on her, encouraging her to "be of good comfort." He reassured her that her faith had worked.

We may be reaching for His garment, for something that we need from Him, but we first need to grab hold of who Jesus really is. Meditate on his essence. Trust in his power, rely on his omniscience, and rest in his compassion today.

---

[2] Matthew 9:20-22 (KJV)

> **Take more time**
>
> Read all of Matthew 9. Meditate on Jesus' love and compassion for people, including you.

Prayer

Thank you for your compassion for me, Jesus. Help me to always remembers Your omnipotence.

17

How I'm Like My Dog...and How I Want to Be

But it is good for me to draw near to God: I have put my trust in the Lord GOD, that I may declare all thy works.

Psalm 73:28 (KJV)

Some time ago we compounded the crazy in our house by adding a fourth furry friend to the family. The dynamic at that time became two parents, three kids, two cats, and two dogs. The new puppy was quite an adjustment.

My husband and I hadn't dealt with the joys and trials of a puppy in a long time, since our good girl, Maggie, was far past that stage. Enter a sweet, yellow lab mix we both couldn't resist. We named him Rico, and when he was five months old, weighing fifty-two pounds, I started reflecting on some lessons he'd taught me in his short life—lessons about who I am and who I want to be.

Rico was not 100% house-trained. He learned quickly, but, as most puppies do, he sometimes had "accidents" in the house. The most frustrating thing about potty training a dog is going a couple of days without any puddles or unpleasant surprises, getting excited about the breakthrough, then walking into the kitchen to find another mess. Three steps forward and two steps back in the process is discouraging.

While it might be the most unusual comparison I've ever made, Rico's shortcomings remind me of myself. I've been a Christ-follower for a long time. I ought to know how this whole thing works, right? I know what sin is, and I should know how to avoid it. But do I always do the right thing? No. I make mistakes just like Rico. Maybe (definitely) not *just* like his mistakes, but I can easily find myself in a stinky situation when I'm not Christ-like in my words, thoughts, or actions. This reality made me want to give Rico a little grace, as Jesus does for me time and time again.

There is at least one way I aspire to be like my dog, though. You see, he is always by my side. If I'm on the couch, he's on the couch. If I'm working in the kitchen, he's in the kitchen. He is a loyal, steadfast companion. He likes to be near me.

The Bibles says, "Draw nigh to God, and he will draw nigh to you."[1] When we nudge in close to the Father, he tucks in close to us right back. May I strive to stay near Him and never leave His side. Drawing close to God through reading the Word, praying, and meditating on Him is how I learn to be more like Him and avoid those "messes" that my sin

---

[1] James 4:8a (KJV)

causes. May I be even more loyal to the Lord than my dog is to me.

 Take more time

Christ is merciful to us when we make mistakes, but we must still strive to avoid sin. Read Romans 6 to understand why.

Prayer

Train me, Lord, to be obedient to You. Keep me close to Your side. Thank you for Your mercy.

18

What's Your Motivation?

But God commendeth his love toward us, in that, while we were yet sinners, Christ died for us.

Romans 5:8 (KJV)

An actor looks at his script for the first time and begins to read a scene from the second act. Because he jumped into the middle of the plot, he doesn't have enough knowledge of the character's backstory and mindset to perform the role believably. He can only infer the correct emotions based on the dialogue.

"What's my motivation?" the actor asks the director. "How did my character get to this point in his journey? What's his story?"

As Christians, we are instructed to do some pretty big things. The Bible says, "Thou shalt love the Lord thy God with all thy heart, and with all thy soul, and with all thy strength, and with all thy mind; and thy neighbour as thyself."[1] Of course, we do this with the help of the Holy Spirit, but as we strive to

---

[1] Luke 10:27 (KJV)

live out this verse, it helps to look at our motivation. Why do we love, serve, and obey Him? What pushes us to keep going?

The Word makes our motivation clear; "We love him, because he first loved us."[2]

He loves us! That's what should motivate us more than anything to follow Him. Especially since we didn't have to earn His love, and we certainly didn't deserve it.

Whenever the journey seems hard and you find yourself asking *why should I* do this or *why should I* do that, remember your motivation; He loves you. The God of the universe loves you unconditionally, and that's enough to keep you going.

---

[2] I John 4:19 (KJV)

> **Take more time**
>
> Do you know the old hymn "Oh, How I Love Jesus"? If you do, sing it to Him. If you don't, take a moment and find a rendition online that you enjoy.

Prayer

Thank You for being love to us. Thank You, Jesus, for Your perfect example. Help us to always remember Your sacrifice.

19

A List for Guiding Your Thoughts

And do not be conformed to this world, but be transformed by the renewing of your mind, that you may prove what is that good and acceptable and perfect will of God.

Romans 12:2 (KJV)

We are bombarded by information all the time, from every direction. Much of it is useful and valuable, but much of it can be harmful to us mentally, emotionally, and spiritually. How do we sort through all the information and guide our thoughts toward the positive?

Philippians 4:8 tells us, and it's a verse I need constantly. If I were going to tattoo scripture on my arm, this would be a helpful one to have. Since I'm not going to do that, I rely on the Holy Spirit to write it on my heart.

"Finally, brethren, whatsoever things are true, whatsoever things are honest, whatsoever things are just, whatsoever things are pure, whatsoever things are lovely, whatsoever things are of good report; if there be any virtue, and if there be any praise, think on these things."[1]

I love that we have a checklist of sorts, for the kinds of things we should think about. Here's another way to break it down. We should spend our mental energy on things that are:

- True
- Honest
- Just
- Pure
- Lovely
- Of good report
- Virtuous
- Praiseworthy

I admit, many things I spend my focus on during the day don't fit into one of these categories. So often, I find myself reading "news" stories that do nothing but leave me sad or angry. There are few things in the news "of good report," and certainly not much on television or in movies is "virtuous." I'm guilty of spending half an hour reading arguments on social media, which are certainly not "praiseworthy," between people I don't even know. It's a disgusting waste of time, and it's difficult to discern if the information we are getting from various sources is even "true" and "honest."

When we fill our brains with the opposite of

---

[1] Philippians 4:8 (KJV)

this verse—dishonest, sinful, condemnable things—it influences the way we act and think. So, here's what I want us to remember; It's OKAY to shut out the negative influences. Take a break from social media, turn off the news, and politely tell trash-talking people that you have other things to do. Then seek out something "pure," or "lovely," or "praiseworthy" to think on. GUARD YOUR MIND!

Another takeaway from Philippians 4:8 is a lesson on how we should think about people. Instead of focusing on people's faults (and yes, I'm talking to myself as a spouse), let's practice "thinking on" the things that are lovely in people. We need to make a conscious effort to *not* think on the gossipy things we hear, and to focus on all the *good* things we know to be true about them.

Use Philippians 4:8 as a checklist for what you should allow into your mind. Ask yourself, "Is it true? Is it pure? Is it praiseworthy, etc.?" It's not an easy thing, but with practice and the Lord's help, we can improve our thought life.

> **Take more time**
>
> Write down the list for guiding your thoughts from Philippians 4:8 and post it where you will see it regularly—bathroom mirror, the sun visor of your car, the refrigerator. Or make it your phone's home screen. Remind yourself often how God wants us to think.

Prayer

Thank you, Jesus, for such clear instructions. Help me to keep my focus on things that honor You.

20

Where Will You Find Yourself Next?

Now unto him that is able to do exceeding abundantly above all that we ask or think, according to the power that worketh in us, Unto him be glory in the church by Christ Jesus throughout all ages, world without end. Amen.

Ephesians 3:20-21 (KJV)

Do you know the Bible speaks of teleportation?

In the eighth chapter of Acts, we see believers fleeing persecution. One of those brave believers was a deacon named Philip. He fled Jerusalem, then traveled to Samaria where he preached until receiving a new assignment from the Lord. He was instructed by an angel to go south to the road that goes "down from Jerusalem unto Gaza, which is desert."[1]

Philip obeyed, and when he reached the road to Gaza, he saw a man sitting in a chariot and reading aloud from the book of Isaiah. Philip revealed Christ

---

[1] Acts 8:27

to the man, who was from Ethiopia, through the Old Testament Scriptures, and he believed. Then they traveled in the chariot to a body of water where Philip baptized the man.

Here's where the teleportation comes in. The Bible says, "And when they were come up out of the water, the Spirit of the Lord caught away Philip, that the eunuch saw him no more: and he went on his way rejoicing. But Philip was found at Azotus: and passing through he preached in all the cities, till he came to Caesarea."[2]

Azotus is the modern-day city of Ashdod, probably an hour-long walk from where Philip had been. The Holy Spirit supernaturally transported Philip to another city. Philip teleported! That might not be the right terminology from a spiritual standpoint, but I think it's the best word in our vocabulary to describe it.

The Scripture doesn't tell us why Philip was caught away, but the story teaches me this: God can move me where He wants me to be, when He wants me to be there, by any means He chooses, when I seek to follow HIS will.

I think this amazing story also teaches us these three concepts.

1.) Be excited for what the Lord could do at any moment! Always anticipate that He can take you somewhere new! A new place of

---

[2] Acts 8:39-40 (KJV)

ministry may be closer than you realize.

2.) Work hard and be obedient. The supernatural help with Philip's journey came only after he had already walked a long way and had completed his mission to witness to the Ethiopian eunuch. You must be faithful in the job to which God has called you first, before your calling will be expanded to other territories.

3.) God is not bound by our idea of time. If He has a job for you to do, He can put you on a fast track if He wants, so don't be discouraged if things don't happen as quickly as you think they should. Trust in His timing.

How exciting it is to serve a God that can do the seemingly impossible! He loves us, and He will accomplish His plan for us, if we allow ourselves to be used. You never know when you might find yourself saying, "How did I wind up here?" and thanking the Lord for His help along the journey.

> **Take more time**
>
> Search Genesis 5 and 2 Kings 2 to learn about two men who were teleported in a different way than Philip was in the book of Acts.

Prayer

God, help me to trust in your timing. Help me understand that You have a perfect plan and You will get me where I need to be to fulfill Your purpose. Thank You for being my faithful guide.

21

The Clear Glass Mosaic

Let your light so shine before men, that they may see your good works, and glorify your Father which is in heaven.

Matthew 5:16 (KJV)

It was a *blah* day. An Ecclesiastes 1 day, if you know what I mean. Emotions crept up, and I felt suddenly purposeless, or as if all my purposes weren't meaningful enough, although I knew it wasn't true.

I stood waiting for my frozen dinner to finish in the microwave when a favorite possession caught my eye—a piece of artwork in a wooden frame, an image of a bluebird on a branch, made out differently shaped and sized pieces of clear glass held together with grout. My husband bought the mosaic for me at a craft fair after I admired it but talked myself out of buying it.

The art hangs from a little chain, on a hook underneath my kitchen cabinet, flat against the wall because it's the only place I could find to hang it. I studied it, then looked up at the half circle window near the top of the vaulted ceiling in my kitchen.

"Ooh, I wonder if it could go up there? That would be pretty!" I thought.

The microwave had five minutes to go, enough time to put in a hook and move the artwork, if I could reach high enough.

On a whim, I stood on the window seat and reached my arm high. Way too short.

I went to the garage and got a step ladder, lugged it into the house, positioned it in front of the window and climbed to the top. Nowhere close.

I thought of putting a chair on the window seat and climbing on top to reach. Way too dangerous, and the window seat wasn't wide enough anyway.

The microwave beeped, and I still hadn't accomplished what my manic brain had determined should happen in that period of time. I held the artwork in different places near the window, trying different homes since my original idea had failed. Testing it out over the window valance, I said to myself aloud, "No, that won't work. It's made to let the light shine through."

There it was. That was the lesson.

The entire episode of me standing in the window seat and dragging a step ladder from the garage, when I had only intended to warm some turkey and mashed sweet potatoes, was for me to get a message about my own purpose.

It's made to the let the light shine through.

I cried. My ho-hum, feeling-good-for-nothing day was instantly transformed. I have a purpose, and it's simple. I'm made to let the light of Jesus shine through me. Just like a clear glass mosaic is more beautiful when the sunlight pours through it, I can show those around me how much more beautiful life is with the love of Christ. Even if I don't feel like I'm doing a good job, that's my purpose. It's every believer's purpose. Life isn't meaningless. We're made to let the light shine through.

 Take more time

Spend some time in the book of John reading about the light we have to shine as believers: John 1:4-5; John 8:12; John 9:5; John 12:35-37.

Prayer

Lord, there are days when my light feels dull. Help me shine brightly for You. Thank you for being the Source of Light in my life.

22

Breath

And the LORD God formed man of the dust of the ground, and breathed into his nostrils the breath of life; and man became a living soul.

Genesis 2:7 (KJV)

It's easy to understand that breathing is necessary for life. God's design for all creatures includes standard functions, including respiration.

As a child, I had mild asthma. Throughout my youth, asthma episodes were minor nuisances occasionally brought on by physical activity. Fast-forward to age twenty-six. I hadn't needed an inhaler in years until hormonal changes during pregnancy brought my asthma back with a vengeance. After three babies, the condition is still a regular part of my life, especially when I have a cold. And I've come to realize, there is nothing like the relief of taking a complete, lung-filling, complication-free breath after an episode of breathing difficulty. It is miraculous, so extraordinarily wonderful. It makes me grateful and in awe.

Just as we couldn't understand love if there

were no evil, or appreciate the beauty of life without pain, I never appreciated and understood the awesomeness of one clear, deep breath—until the first time I struggled to breathe as an adult.

The difference between struggling to breathe and breathing freely is like the difference between being spiritually lost and being saved. Before Christ, we were existing but fighting for air. After Christ, we breathe deeply and experience the fullness and completeness of life in Him.

Every living soul is born of the breath of God, but every soul does not automatically have the breath of eternal life. That comes from accepting Him as Savior and surrendering your life to Him. Have you made that decision? Are you breathing easy today?

> **Take more time**
>
> Read John 20:2 to learn about another type of life-giving breath.

Prayer

Thank you, God, for physical and spiritual breath. You are the breath of life, and I am made alive in You. Help me share the story of Your life-giving love with others.

23

If My Bible Disappeared

Your word is a lamp to my feet and a light to my path.

Psalm 119:105 (ESV)

Driving with my smartphone in my lap, I reached for it over and over as if it might somehow run away. Every stoplight and stop sign was a chance to check for notifications. I became aware of my need for validation in the form of little red circles on a screen, and I had to admit something I'd known for a while; I'm addicted to my phone. I never want to be without it.

The rest of the drive was spent contemplating other things I treasure, things I don't want to live without. I thought about the Bible. What if I had to live without it? If for some reason my Bible, and my Bible app, suddenly disappeared from my life, how much of it would I have hidden away in my heart?

God provided His Word to teach us about Him and to guide us in righteousness. The Bible is more accessible and more available throughout the world now than it has been at any time in history.

Although in some parts of the world, people put themselves at great risk by owning a Bible. Knowing that I don't appreciate the ease of access to God's Word like I should, I have to question how I'd be affected if it were taken away. Would the fact that I've memorized John 3:16 fulfill me? Would the Lord's Prayer and Psalm 23 be enough? How would I hunger for it and grieve over it if I couldn't have it?

I believe the Lord will preserve His word, but it was good to think about how life would change if the Bible suddenly vanished and wasn't here to light my path. I imagine I would write down every verse of Scripture I know and pray to remember more. I would probably ask everyone around me what verses they remembered as well.

Thankfully, the Holy Spirit can never be taken away and will always be my Guide, but I pray that God will continue to speak to me through His Word, and that I will treasure it. If the idea of losing the Bible breaks your heart, that's a good thing. We need to revere the Holy Scriptures and commit it to memory, not for fear that it will be taken away, but to allow it to work in our lives.

Take more time

Pick a verse from the Word that you don't already know by heart. Practice it all day until you have it etched into your memory.

Prayer

Thank You for making Your Word available to me. Help me appreciate it for the life-changing gift that it is.

24

Sent Away by Jesus

But ye are a chosen generation, a royal priesthood, an holy nation, a peculiar people; that ye should shew forth the praises of him who hath called you out of darkness into his marvellous light:

1 Peter 2:9 (KJV)

When Jesus was on earth, he did many great and mighty miracles. On more than one occasion, he even confronted the powers of darkness head-on. The Scriptures tell of Jesus rescuing people from literal possession by evil spirits. He was God in flesh, and that was no problem for Him.

One familiar story is the man who lived among the tombs in the country of the Gadarenes.[1] We're told the man was too strong to be bound with chains, and that no one could tame him. He cried day and night, and he cut himself with stones. What a miserable existence! But when he encountered Jesus, his life was instantly transformed. Jesus commanded the devils to leave the man, and they had to obey.

One part of the story that sticks out to me is

---

[1] Mark 5:1-20

found in verses 18 and 19 (KJV):

"And when he (Jesus) was come into the ship, he that had been possessed with the devil prayed him that he might be with him. Howbeit Jesus suffered him not, but saith unto him, Go home to thy friends, and tell them how great things the Lord hath done for thee, and hath had compassion on thee."

The account of the story in Luke is worded this way:

"Now the man out of whom the devils were departed besought him that he might be with him: but Jesus sent him away, saying, Return to thine own house, and shew how great things God hath done unto thee."[2]

This man, whom Jesus rescued from horrifying circumstances, asked Jesus for one more thing—just to be with him. There weren't any conditions to the request. The man didn't ask where Jesus was going or where He might be staying. It didn't matter; he simply wanted to stay near him.

I can't help but wonder if there was fear in the man's heart that the demons would return to possess him again. Maybe he wanted Jesus nearby for protection. Or maybe the request was solely a response of adoration for the one who had redeemed him. Either way, he was wise in wanting to stay with Jesus. Where is there a better place to be? But Jesus denied his request. He told him he must go home and tell others what had happened to him. Jesus sent him

---

[2] Luke 8:38-39a (KJV)

away, with a mission. How many people learned about the Messiah through the testimony of this man?

We too were bound by the devil. Our spirits, like the poor man in our passage, could not be tamed by anyone. No matter how good we may have seemed from the outside, before Christ, we were possessed by our sin. Then Jesus arrived, and now we've been transformed. He delivered us from the powers of darkness.

Jesus has done a great thing for us, and though we may be tempted to bask in our redemption, we are compelled to go and tell what He has done. He had compassion on all of us and gave His life so that we can have fullness of life here and eternity with Him. That's worth sharing.

I used to struggle with depression and anxiety. Now I don't. God healed me, and I think that's something people should know, so they understand there is hope. That's something I need to "go tell."

Fortunately, when we go tell, it is different than it was for "the man out of whom the devils departed." Jesus goes with us. We don't have to leave Him behind in order to share the story of His great compassion with others. May God make us bold to tell "how great things the Lord hath done."

Take more time

Read John 8:31-36, then search your heart. Do you truly have the freedom Jesus speaks of in verses 32 and 36?

Prayer

Thank You, Jesus, for breaking every chain of sin. Give me boldness to tell the world what You've done for me.

25

Invitation Etiquette

And the Spirit and the bride say, "Come!" And let him who hears say, "Come!" And let him who thirsts come. Whoever desires, let him take the water of life freely.

Revelation 21:17 (NKJV)

You open the mailbox and there's a card addressed to you. Someone is throwing the party of the century, and you're invited to attend! Whether you can make it or not, an invitation has been extended, and the sender deserves a response.

Jesus has extended many kinds of invitations. Some of them, even believers ignore. What will you do with your invitations? Respond affirmatively; say no thank you; or, ignore them?

Let's look at just a few of the things He invites us to do, from the examples of Scripture:

1.) **Be saved**. Isaiah 55:3: "Incline your ear, and **come** unto me: hear, and your soul shall live; and I will make an everlasting covenant with you..."

2.) **Rest.** Matthew 11:28: "**Come** unto me, all ye that labour and are heavy laden, and I will give you rest."

3.) **Be satisfied.** John 7:37-39: "In the last day, that great day of the feast, Jesus stood and cried, saying, If any man thirst, let him **come** unto me, and drink. He that believeth on me, as the scripture hath said, out of his belly shall flow rivers of living water."

4.) **Fellowship with Him.** John 21:12: "Jesus saith unto them, **Come** and dine..."

5.) **Inherit.** Matthew 25:34: "Then shall the King say unto them on his right hand, **Come**, ye blessed of my Father, inherit the kingdom prepared for you from the foundation of the world."

Jesus invites us to come and be saved, rest and be satisfied in Him, fellowship with Him, and inherit eternal life. What is your response? Please be polite. Don't ignore any of these special invitations.

This devotion was adapted from the sermon notes of a message written and delivered by Rev. Bobby Norman.

Take more time

Read the parable of the feast in Luke 14:15-24 and think about the most important event you've ever attended or hosted. No event can compare to the invitations we have from Jesus.

Prayer

Dear God, thank you for the wondrous invitations You've extended. You are a gracious and generous Lord. Help us to respond affirmatively to everything You've invited us to do as Your children.

26

Time to Look Back

*Oh, taste and see that the LORD is good;
Blessed is the man who trusts in Him!*

Psalm 34:8 (NKJV)

There are many verses in scripture that warn us *not* to look back. Jesus said, "No man, having put his hand to the plough, and looking back, is fit for the kingdom of God."[1] This reference to looking back means longing for an old lifestyle or turning away from the calling of God. But looking back in the right way is a good thing!

If you need a dose of joy in your day, spend some time taking inventory of the blessings God has poured out. Look back over the course of your life and see from where He's brought you. We sometimes take for granted the ways he keeps us from day to day, but if we look back over the span of several years, it is mind-blowing and obvious what the Lord has worked.

I recently found myself reflecting on a

---

[1] Luke 9:62 (KJV)

conversation I had with my husband before he and I started dating. We were just "work friends" then, and he was admittedly a non-believer. I asked him if he was concerned about what would happen to him after death, to which he replied, "Not really."

This memory almost made me shout for joy! Why? Because now my husband has been a believer for years and is a minister telling other people about Jesus. Who but God can do that?

We need to remember where we came from, not lamenting for the "good old days" but praising God for leading us toward His purpose.

Read the words of Moses from Deuteronomy 6:10-12 (NKJV): "So it shall be, when the LORD your God brings you into the land of which He swore to your fathers, to Abraham, Isaac, and Jacob, to give you large and beautiful cities which you did not build, houses full of all good things, which you did not fill, hewn-out wells which you did not dig, vineyards and olive trees which you did not plant—when you have eaten and are full—then beware, lest you forget the LORD who brought you out of the land of Egypt, from the house of bondage."

He was saying: Don't forget where God brought you from! None of what you have is by your own hand! God did it!

> **Take more time**
>
> Take time to reflect today. What has God done that amazes you when you look back at your life? Maybe write down some of the unexpected blessings He's given.

Prayer

Thank you, Lord, for guiding me, each step of the way. I am undeserving of the blessings You've provided. Help me recognize each of them and never fail to give You praise.

27

The Real Root of All Evil

"And you shall know the truth, and the truth shall make you free."

John 8:32 (NKJV)

It is often said that money is the root of all evil. Indeed, the Scriptures tell us that the *love* of money is the root of all evil. But we understand there are many sins that have nothing to do with money, so we must look at the verse in context.

"For the love of money is the root of all evil: which while some coveted after, they have erred from the faith, and pierced themselves through with many sorrows."[1] Here we see money was the root of all the evils of those who coveted after it and allowed it to compromise the tenets of their faith.

There is, however, another portion of Scripture in the New Testament that I believe explains the cause of ALL evil in the world. It seems too simple that there is a singular problem with mankind that causes us to sin, but the first chapter of

---

[1] 1 Timothy 6:10

Romans provides a powerful and concise explanation.

"Because that which may be known of God is manifest in them; for God hath shewed it unto them. For the invisible things of him from the creation of the world are clearly seen, being understood by the things that are made, even his eternal power and Godhead; so that they are without excuse: Because that, when they knew God, they glorified him not as God, neither were thankful; but became vain in their imaginations, and their foolish heart was darkened."[2]

There is no such thing as an atheist. I find it hard to believe that anyone could look at the beauty and majesty of creation and arrive at the conclusion that it is all a serendipitous result of cosmic happenstance. We have the evidence of God the creator right in front of us, so there is no excuse for unbelief.

So, what is the cause of evil? Not glorifying God as God and not being thankful. (I suppose that really is two causes, but I think they go together.) Along with that comes worshipping and serving the creature more than the Creator, which brings us back to the love of money—a "thing" that people have created and tried to elevate above God.

In this same chapter, verses 26 through 31 list some of the sins prompted by the failure to honor God as the Omnipotent, Omniscient, Omnipresent Creator.

---

[2] Romans 1:20-21

We sin when we fail to recognize His creative power and His authority over all creation. I believe much of the moral decline of our society can be attributed to the theory of evolution being widely embraced as scientific fact. People have bent and stretched the definition of science for the express purpose of denying the Creator.

While not honoring God as Creator is the starting point of sin for many, others may espouse the idea of Intelligent Design and still fail to honor God by not following His divine instructions outlined for us in the Bible.

Now that we understand the cause of sin, at a base level, what is the antithesis of a sinful life? Romans 1 gives us the answer for that, too!

Verse 16 says: "For I am not ashamed of the gospel of Christ: for it is the power of God unto salvation to every one that believeth; to the Jew first, and also to the Greek." And verse 17 delivers the final answer: "For therein is the righteousness of God revealed from faith to faith: as it is written, The just shall live by faith." (For further study, the last part of verse 17 is a reference to Habakkuk 2:4.)

How beautifully the Word of God fits together! It doesn't condemn and just point out the weaknesses of man. It mercifully gives us instruction for how not to fail. The antithesis of a sinful life— one of wickedness, deceitfulness, envy, pride, etc.— is one of faith in Jesus and the redemption that comes from Him alone.

> **Take more time**
>
> Read Romans 1:20 again and keep reading to the end of the chapter. It will give you more insight about the root of evil in humanity, so you can prevail against it.

Prayer

Forgive me, Jesus, when I fail to acknowledge Your divinity. Thank You for Your Word that reveals the truth of who You are.

28

Praying from the Word

And this is the confidence that we have in him, that, if we ask any thing according to his will, he heareth us: And if we know that he hear us, whatsoever we ask, we know that we have the petitions that we desired of him.

1 John 5:14-15 (KJV)

God speaks to us through Scripture, but have you ever considered using the Bible to communicate with Him as well?

We are given the model prayer by Our Lord in Matthew 6 and in Luke 11. Certainly, there is power in reciting this prayer every day with a sincere heart, and all our prayers should center around four words from the Lord's Prayer, "Thy will be done." But I'd like to present more verses that can be used in your conversation with the Lord.

From the Old Testament, we can use many of the Psalms, from the heart of King David, as our own plea to God. Here are just a few I've connected as a personal prayer.

Let the words of my mouth, and the meditation of my heart, be acceptable in thy sight, O LORD, my strength, and my redeemer[1]. Create in me a clean heart, O God; and renew a right spirit within me.[2] Teach me to do thy will; for thou art my God: thy spirit is good; lead me into the land of uprightness.[3]

From the New Testament, we can use Paul's prayer for the church at Philippi, found in Philippians 1:9-11, as the basis of a personal prayer.

May my love abound still more and more in knowledge and all discernment, that I may approve the things that are excellent, that I may be sincere and without offense till the day of Christ, being filled with the fruits of righteousness which are by Jesus Christ, to the glory and praise of God.

What more can we ask for in life than to grow in love for the glory of God? This is my sincere prayer.

The Word is full of examples of righteous requests we can make. Thankfully, we also have the Holy Spirit to guide us in our communication with God; we have Jesus as our intercessor with the

---

[1] Psalm 19:14
[2] Psalm 51:10
[3] Psalm 143:10

Father, and there is no required formula or specific liturgy needed.

Whatever format you use, take time to talk to God today.

> **Take more time**
>
> Search the Scriptures for your own prayer prompts or write down the ones provided here for easy reference.

Prayer

Our Father in heaven, hallowed be Your name. Your kingdom come. Your will be done on earth as it is in heaven. Give us this day our daily bread. And forgive us our debts, as we forgive our debtors. And do not lead us into temptation, but deliver us from the evil one. For Yours is the kingdom and the power and the glory forever. Amen.[4]

---

[4] Matthew 6:9-13 (NKJV)

29

Schools of Fish and Jesus-Followers

Holy Father, keep through thine own name those whom thou hast given me, that they may be one, as we are.

John 17:11b (KJV)

One of my favorite places is a spot on the bank of a canal that connects the Intracoastal Waterway and the Atlantic. I enjoy watching the schools of little fish next to the bank as they glide and dart in perfect unison. They scatter in every direction when a bug taps the surface, then immediately come back together. Watching them makes me think about the Church, because I've come to realize that Christ-followers must be part of a unified body for some of the same reasons fish swim in schools.

Fish swim in schools 1.) To help keep them safe, 2.) To find food, and 3.) To find a mate.

As believers, we need each other. We need to be unified. And believe it or not, the instinctive motivations of fish align with the spiritual benefits of being united with other Jesus-Followers.

To Keep Safe

When believers are unified in a church family, it provides spiritual safety. We are called to hold one another accountable. The church family is our spiritual "school," and not only do we protect one another from straying, we can guide each other in the faith.

- "Brethren, if a man be overtaken in a fault, ye which are spiritual, restore such an one in the spirit of meekness; considering thyself, lest thou also be tempted. Bear ye one another's burdens, and so fulfil the law of Christ."[1]

- "Brethren, if any of you do err from the truth, and one convert him; Let him know, that he which converteth the sinner from the error of his way shall save a soul from death, and shall hide a multitude of sins."[2]

The body of Christ should operate as a cohesive unit to help protect individual believers from spiritual danger.

---

[1] Galatians 6:1-2 (KJV)
[2] James 5:19-20 (KJV)

To Find Food

We join with other believers to receive spiritual food—that is sustenance that helps us grow in the faith.

- "Not forsaking the assembling of ourselves together, as the manner of some is; but exhorting one another: and so much the more, as ye see the day approaching."[3]

- "Let the word of Christ dwell in you richly in all wisdom; teaching and admonishing one another in psalms and hymns and spiritual songs, singing with grace in your hearts to the Lord."[4]

We come together—teaching, preaching, and singing—to be fed spiritually.

To Find a Mate

For a marriage to be optimally successful, a man and woman must be aligned spiritually; in other words, part of the same "school."

- "Be ye not unequally yoked together with unbelievers: for what fellowship hath

---

[3] Hebrews 10:25 (KJV)
[4] Colossians 3:16 (KJV)

righteousness with unrighteousness? and what communion hath light with darkness?"[5]

***

Think about how much we can accomplish when believers are in sync with one another, like that little school of fish! Believers, join together and keep swimming!

 Take more time

Read another passage about unity among believers, 1 Corinthians 1:10.

Prayer

Thank You, God, for speaking to us through Your creation. Help us to always see and hear the lessons You have for us.

---

[5] 2 Corinthians 6:14 (KJV)

30

Are You Where You Thought You'd Be?

In all thy ways acknowledge him, and he shall direct thy paths.

Proverbs 3:6 (KJV)

Out of all the people in this big, wide world, I imagine there are a few who grew up to live exactly the life their high school selves imagined. Maybe there are some whose ten-year plan was realized to the letter. The dreams of their youth played out exactly as they had envisioned. Maybe a few. A very, very few. For most of us, that's just not how it works. We grow, our plans change, and life happens.

Whether your plans didn't work out or you had no clear path to begin with, chances are, you can look back at your life with some measure of amusement and perhaps awe. "How did I wind up here?" you might ask yourself. And for the Spirit-filled believer, the answer is obvious.

Jeremiah 29:11 (ESV) says, "For I know the plans I have for you, declares the LORD, plans for welfare and not for evil, to give you a future and a hope."

I can see them now. What were invisible road signs at the time saying, "Turn Here." God planted these markers along my path, long before I started walking it. He knew the plan.

In my career there have been many turning points. Like when I was an eighteen-year-old part-time filing clerk in an insurance office and my boss offered to pay for me to take classes to get my agent's license. I couldn't have known that his kindness would put me on a career path that would help me enter the corporate world and eventually leave the insurance field for a job in Information Technology. But God knew.

In my early twenties, I couldn't see that this cool guy—whose friendship I once described as the most platonic relationship I'd ever had with a guy—would eventually become my husband and the father to my three children. But there was a singular moment when a spark ignited and changed the course of my life. I didn't recognize it right away. But God knew.

After many unexpected turns, I'm glad I'm not the one in control. I certainly never envisioned I'd be here on this writing journey, and I love it. I'm so grateful for it.

One of the many wonderful things about being a child of God is being able to trust in His providence. You can trust him with the future. Go ahead and make plans, but leave room for holy detours. And never doubt where He can take you.

If you're not where you thought you'd be in life, there are two appropriate responses. Either thank God for all the turning points along the way, or be glad and trust that He's not finished leading yet.

 Take more time

Read Ecclesiastes 3:1-8 and meditate on the different seasons of life through which God has brought you.

Prayer

Lord, I trust You with my life. I trust You to lead me where You want me to go. Thank You for being my Guide.

Closing Prayer

Come unto me, all ye that labour and are heavy laden, and I will give you rest

Matthew 11:28 (KJV)

Lord, I'm so tired today—feeling like there's no way I can possibly be all the things I need to be, to all the people who need me; feeling like a mental, emotional, or physical breakdown is soon-coming, and it's a toss-up as to which happens first.

Then the guilt comes. How can I complain about being tired when there are people battling cancer today? How can I complain about having so much to do when there are people longing for children to keep them busy and hoping for jobs to help pay their bills? Then I hear You whisper, "It's okay."

There is therefore now no condemnation to them which are in Christ Jesus, who walk not after the flesh, but after the Spirit.[1]

Thank you, Father.

---

[1] Romans 8:1 (KJV)

But I don't want the world to see my rotten attitude and my down-trodden expression. I represent You! What if they see the way I struggle today and get the wrong idea about Your Goodness?

Another whisper.

But they that wait upon the LORD shall renew their strength; they shall mount up with wings as eagles; they shall run, and not be weary; and they shall walk, and not faint.[2]

Thank you, Lord, for knowing what I need.

And now that You've given me Grace in exchange for my guilt, and Strength in exchange for me weakness, now, and only now, can I focus on serving those around me, and on being Your hands and feet.

Lord, help me fulfill the commission. Let me not get in the way. Help me live Philippians 4:13, because it's true! I *can* do all things through Christ who gives me strength. And now that this truth has been proven in me, let me share it with someone who hasn't quite caught on yet.

Let me be redemption and not judgement.

---

[2] Isaiah 40:31 (KJV)

Let me be truth and not confusion.

Let me be hope and not disillusionment.

Let me be a help and not a hindrance.

Let me build up and not tear down.

No. Matter. How. Tired. I. Am.

Your Grace is sufficient.

In my weakness, Your strength is demonstrated.

Let me slip off the yoke of the world and follow Your lead.

You are El Shaddai, and I am Yours.

Amen.

AUTHOR'S NOTE

I sincerely hope you were encouraged by this book. If it ministered to you in some way, I'd love to hear about it. Please reach out to me through my website, where you can also sign up for my email newsletter, read my latest blog posts, and find out about upcoming books. I'd also enjoy connecting with you on social media. Look for me on Facebook, Twitter, and Instagram.

If you enjoyed *Timeout for Jesus*, please consider recommending it by writing a review on Goodreads, BookBub, and Amazon, or other online retailers.

Thank you so much for reading!

-Heather

www.heathernormansmith.com

www.ingramcontent.com/pod-product-compliance
Lightning Source LLC
Chambersburg PA
CBHW052100070526
44584CB00017B/2264